DIALOGUES

OF THE SOUL

AND MORTAL SELF

IN TIME

Books by Jane Roberts

THE SETH MATERIAL

SETH SPEAKS:
The Eternal Validity of the Soul

THE EDUCATION OF OVERSOUL 7

THE NATURE OF PERSONAL REALITY:
A Seth Book

ADVENTURES IN CONSCIOUSNESS:
An Introduction to Aspect Psychology

DIALOGUES OF THE SOUL
AND MORTAL SELF IN TIME

PSYCHIC POLITICS:
An Aspect Psychology Book

THE "UNKNOWN" REALITY:
A Seth Book (Volume 1)

THE WORLD VIEW OF PAUL CÉZANNE

THE AFTERDEATH JOURNAL
OF AN AMERICAN PHILOSOPHER

In Preparation:
THE "UNKNOWN" REALITY:
A Seth Book (Volume 2)

THE NATURE OF THE PSYCHE:
A Seth Book

DIALOGUES
OF THE SOUL
AND MORTAL SELF
IN TIME

by

Jane Roberts

drawings by
Robert F. Butts

PRENTICE-HALL, INC., Englewood Cliffs, N. J.

4|11

Library of Congress Cataloging in Publication Data
Roberts, Jane.
    Dialogues of the soul and mortal self in time.
    Poems.
    I. Title.
PS3568.02387D5   811'.5'4   75-12631
ISBN 0-13-208546-1 pbk

PREFACE: POETRY and TRANSCENDENT EXPERIENCE

Who needs poetry? All of us do. Poetry has always been the voice of the inner self, the carrier of revelations, dreams, and visions that often defy expression in ordinary prose.

Poetry and altered states of consciousness have always gone hand in hand. It's when our perceptions are most vivid and striking that we break out into song, and resort to rhythm, written or spoken. It's whenever we're transported by emotion or insight that we leap beyond usual language use, to seek expression in a form that can transcend the seeming boundaries of noun and verb, subject and predicate. When we are what we perceive, then we turn to poetry to express the knowledge that astounds and scandalizes the more pedestrian orientation of our prose-tuned minds.

"I love you"—that can be written in a sentence where "you" and "I" are separated as much as united by the word "love." But when emotion goes beyond that, when "I," "love," and "you" are all equal, experienced in a flash of transcendent unity, then the prose statement with its built-in structural separations just won't do. We need poetry instead— rich symbolism, rhythms, associations, and anything else that will help us express the varied depths of that feeling.

All of us at one time or another have experienced moments in which we outspeed ourselves, when insights about our lives and the nature of reality come so quickly that we can hardly keep track; when we perceive our beings so much more fully than usual that normal expression or explanation seems futile.

Our language even structures our experience. Cause and effect is built into the prose sentence. Often greater realizations can't be shown in that context, without annihilating verbs and nouns altogether, and reuniting them in a different way.

v

But poetry, like dreams, deals with another kind of spiritual or psychic logic that builds upon inner associations and defies our ideas of time and cause and effect. Its truth comes from a different level of consciousness that demands a more multidimensional method of expression.

Transcendent experience automatically seeks that freedom and "accelerated discipline." Odd term. Yet in poetry, perceptions are concentrated; felt as strongly as we can bear them. The writing of poetry puts you in a kind of trance in which focus is brilliantly tuned to one area: All backgrounds of association and knowledge are searched with that in mind, and all superfluous data ignored. For that matter, the state of consciousness in which poetry is written can itself be a transcendent experience and a threshold into still other altered conditions.

The writing of poetry automatically organizes our experience and lives in a different fashion, bringing together our minds, spirits and emotions, and our waking and dreaming selves in a new unified way. There are times, of course, when our transcendent experiences go beyond words, when what we suddenly know defies any kind of translation; when we are so at one with ourselves that expression is not necessary or even desirable.

On other occasions, such events may be interpreted in different terms—biologically, for example, through the cells and molecules, resulting in a "healing" instead of a poem; or through direct action of another sort, culminating in a complete change of direction that alters our lives. A peak experience can involve a sports event, when the body seems to transcend itself, performing with an ease and daring far superior to its usual state.

But here we're considering poetry and transcendent experience, when going beyond ourselves results in an artistically competent poem, or even better, a great one. A richly rewarding spiritual illumination can result in a lousy poem, of course, pedestrian verse, or an embarrassingly gushy one, using clichés all the more jarring in contrast to the uniqueness they're meant to express.

But when poetry "works," the known and seemingly unknown realities of our lives merge into a new symmetry of form, each becoming more by virtue of its connection with the other. The commonplace is endowed with its own originality, seen as itself, for itself; and the rare is perceived as a sparkling segment of an overall pattern that is at once individual, and a part of everything else.

When poetry works, our conscious and unconscious minds know their harmony. More, we learn the basic inadequacy of the phrase, "the conscious mind," because we see that our consciousness is like a light of many colors that sheds its tints and meanings across inner and outer landscapes alike, and in a way, forms each.

We are always translating realities from one framework to another; transient electromagnetic sequences and light spectrums into visions of light and dark, color, size, shape, and motion. The world of objects rises into prominence through our senses, which translate the unknowable into knowable terms. So this life itself may be a three-dimensional living vision that includes all the lovely sense-paraphernalia we know, experienced through one particular lens of consciousness.

But when we turn our consciousness in other directions and view this world off-focus, look at it sidewards, then we perceive different visions. Certainly these must be interpreted, and related to the normal world. Yet many corresponding realities or alternate visions exist, if only we look in the proper directions, and those glimpses of otherness can and should also illuminate the life of sense.

No road of consciousness is dead-ended.

Poetry and art, in general, have always been our way of expressing such other-experiences; those which are superimposed on the world we know and those that, on rare occasions, supersede it.

Truths are often outfitted in the guise of art, where fact and fiction are only versions one of the other, in a different order of events in which the imagination glimpses a deeper reality from which all appearances spring. In *that* framework, all usual rules forsake us, for there a fiction can be more truthful—more real—than a fact; and a fantasy can have a greater effect upon us than a mountain of provable data, and remake the fabric of our lives. Here we are dealing with the secrets of creativity from which physical effects emerge.

Often prose can't bear the strain of that kind of expression. We go beyond its one-order reference and time orientation. Science, like the English language itself, deals with objectification, specialization, and the division of subject and object, perceiver and perceived. Certainly there are advantages in viewing reality in that particular fashion. But the transcendent experience and poetic inspiration involve emotional identification; the antithesis of separation and alienation.

One system *can* enrich the other. I'm happy to know the scientific facts about weather, for example, and how thunderstorms are formed. But when I identify with a raging storm, imaginatively throw in my lot with the great driving energy of the wind, I learn more about myself and nature than I can from any statistical facts or scientific explanations; but it is knowledge of a different kind. I see my psyche reflected in the storm, feel the primeval yet ever new flow of my own passions, and glory in my creaturehood.

The grandeur of earth speaks to us through identification, and when our languages or sciences forget *that*, then we feel ourselves aliens in an objectified world that always seems to exist outside of us and bears no relationship to the reality of our own emotions or subjective experience.

In that regard at least, Percy Shelley's poem "Ode to the West Wind" gives me a more "truthful" picture of a storm and my relationship with the seasons than any number of facts about wind currents, duration of months, or length of growing seasons. But Shelley's truth can't be fitted into the world of facts in the same way that, say, statistics can. Both exist, each valid and each presenting alternate ways of viewing reality.

Poetry, then, uses language differently than prose does.

It deals more fully with images, associations, and rhythm; allows a greater flexibility; and provides a form that is disciplined even while its structure is more open. Even the different arrangement of the words on the page, the stanzas, and the breakup of normal sentences help us to jump over usual assumptions, shake us up and make us think. We don't automatically translate our experience into habitual patterns. Old associations are broken—to some readers, a painful process.

And often the poet may outdo himself, go too far in his desire to be original so that little or nothing is really communicated. The poetry becomes overly esoteric, too divorced from usual experience, strained. This embarrasses us in the same way that we blush for a singer trying to reach a note too high for the voice. You just want the whole thing over with. You collapse with relief when its done. Yet the poor performance is like some orgasm that doesn't quite come off simply because you tried so hard, knowing that it could have been so great.

So often a poem doesn't make it for the same reason. The initial vision was so original that its natural rhythm and follow-through was impeded because the poet wanted the expression to be so right, or lofty, or awe-inspiring.

For poems, like transcendent states, have their climaxes —the peaks of experience in which perception, however briefly, goes beyond itself—and everything is suddenly new, super-real; when it seems that breath will stop and that the world will never be the same again.

These do not have to be events of a cosmic nature. They can instead—and often do—involve heightened consciousness of everyday items or circumstances. But when they happen, we know that we've somehow approached the thresholds of being.

Such transcendent experiences can be initiated by almost anything, but once the event begins it illuminates all portions of our lives. *Dialogues* was triggered almost comically by a trivial enough event. A well-known writer referred to me in a national magazine as middle-aged. His article mentioned my books and ideas, in which all time is seen as simultaneous, and my work was treated quite fairly. But I felt humiliated and furious, and no matter what I told myself intellectually, I couldn't shake the emotional outrage.

I found myself in tears, shouting and swearing vigorously. At the same time I saw the humor of the situation, but this only angered me further. I refused to deny the validity of my emotions, so I went along with them. Yet I was struck by the difference between my intellectual concepts about time and my emotional reaction to it, at least in this instance. The mind haughtily went its way, while the body was faced with its daily encounter with time and the seasons. And here "I" was, caught in this gap of understanding, suspended between mind and body's experience of reality. But "I" was hot, angry, stuffy from crying; so there, anyhow, emotions and corporal sensations held sway.

And how could you reconcile the two? I stood there, blowing my nose, quite clearly aware of three separate lines of awareness: emotional uprushes of hurt and anger; a somewhat detached, amused, intellectual analysis of the situation; and a third line of focus in which I looked "back" with some compassion from another viewpoint on a creature whose experience contained that kind of dilemma. This last level didn't feel either the emotions or the intellectual questions, but was aware of each and not caught up in the problem.

The very next instant the first verse of *Dialogues* sprang fully into my mind. I stopped, somewhat startled, and wrote the lines down. Within an hour and a half, I had the first four long poems. It's as if the three lines of awareness just mentioned each went its own way. "I" identified with the emotional elements (while questioning them at the same time), and in the poem this becomes the voice of the mortal self, who questions the soul. The third line of consciousness —apart, compassionate yet sometimes "tart"—above the dilemmas of mortal existence yet connected with it, becomes the Soul. The poem's narrator seems to be the second line of focus, detached enough to present the scenes and mildly curious as to what would develop as soul and mortal self begin their dialogues.

None of this was consciously considered in usual terms at the time. In fact, only when I began to read my notes over for this preface did I identify that one moment when consciousness showed a triple face as the one in which *Dialogues* was born.

I had no idea that more than a few poems were involved. Then, as I went about my days, *Dialogues* came whole poems at a time, in accelerated states of consciousness in which I wrote sometimes from morning to evening. *Dialogues* and my daily life merged. The quality of my awareness changed to such a degree that the poem was my living experience, and my living experience was the poem.

The dramatic situation set up in the artistic production began to change as the dialogues between mortal self and soul progressed, and the relationship between them altered creatively, and in life. This led, of course, to the resolution of the poem, and to a personal reconciliation.

The visions mentioned in *Dialogues were* visions, literally experienced. These are not meant as simply symbolic statements, then, though symbolism was also strongly involved. I *saw* the rain creature rise up from the rainy walk (Part Two) ; and a light *did* appear in the kitchen. When you read that section, you can call the light anything you want, from a complete hallucination to an apport from one level of consciousness to another, or take it for granted that it was caused by some physical event of which I was ignorant. You can question its reality as physical fact—though I don't—but I insist upon its truth.

Some episodes, such as the out-of-body experiences, were re-created as I wrote the poem. They actually happened earlier and while they were occurring I couldn't describe them. They were imaginatively re-experienced as I wrote, and in a heightened state I was able to feel what was happening at one level and describe it at another.

The same applies to the paper episode. During the original event I was so immersed in the experience, so at-one with the paper that I was no more able to write or speak than it was. As I wrote, the whole thing came back, with great intensity; but this time I was apart from the event enough to describe it.

The writing of *Dialogues*, then, was itself a peak experience, and became a framework that initiated, directed, and organized other transcendent episodes and translated them into an art form. These events had a psychic and psychological basis: questions that bothered me deeply were presented to the soul who then responded either with answers or with objective experiences or visions. The word "psyche" can be used instead of "soul," of course. What is important is the dialogue—in which questions posed at one level of consciousness are answered by another level, and in ways unsuspected by the questioner.

Besides this, certain events suddenly came into focus from the mundane habits and circumstances of daily life; were seized upon for the purposes of the poem and used with its particular questions in mind. A high level of selectivity operated, then, of which I was not consciously aware. The smallest details—a phone call or a jay's squawk—were lifted into brilliant clarity in both physical and symbolic terms.

Just when I wondered, "What next?" something, perhaps a squirrel, would appear out of nowhere—a psychological apport; an omen suddenly not just significant but significant to me and no one else. Oh personal universe! Here was no distant, uncaring objectified world, but one in which all messages were perceived, all questions in one way or another answered.

But only if—a big if—you accepted the framework. Squirrels clamor about the oak tree outside my study window all the time, so certainly they didn't come out of a physical nowhere. Yet they did spring from a *psychological* nowhere into significance and reality. They'd always been there, but now their being *there* and my being *here* was united in a new, charged relationship.

We're taught that we must stay clear, that such identification is dangerous, primitive; that only primitive tribes (who don't survive) have that kind of relationship with nature. Yet the personal universe offers a sense of psychic belonging that releases our natural abilities, encourages our strengths, and restores our creative vitality.

For the three months that I worked on *Dialogues*, for example, my inner and outer worlds balanced each other so delicately and yet securely that their complementary nature was everywhere apparent. The living webworks that connect our waking and dreaming experience *showed*; they glimmered and glittered to be followed back and forth between the self and soul's single-double worlds. The translation of such experience into an art form is quite apparent; from the individual poems you can see what questions asked by the mortal self triggered a given transcendent experience, and then follow its expression in the next verse.

I was so completely involved on so many levels that sometimes it was difficult to tell if I was writing the poem or it was writing me, because certainly it focused all of my experience and attention.

This applied even in the simplest of terms. I almost always hibernate (symbolically at least) in winter, and the dreary days always leave me longing for spring. That year, through the poetry, my habitual feelings were overcome.

The same kind of reconciliation happened in other instances. One of our pet cats died, and my sorrow, while felt to the fullest, was transformed through the poetry into something else, some transcendent triumph as I wrote "A Lyric to Rooney." The entire passage was written the day the cat died. The minor household tragedy let me put death in perspective, my parents' by hindsight and my own by projection.

As I followed the soul's instructions, allowing myself to feel my emotions as directly as possible, I began to feel their reflection and expression in my body in a new way. Emotions that I'd considered contradictory in the past were bridged by others until I saw them as orchestrations in which each emotion was valid and as "good" as the other.

The questions asked by the mortal self are questions asked at one time or another by each of us, but the dialogue form was not consciously chosen because it was an excellent writing technique, and the questions asked were intensely personal. I wasn't pretending to speak for others, or taking a literary stance. Those were *my* questions, and I received personal answers in return, and visions that were entirely my own.

Yet while we are alive in creaturehood I think that we carry on a continuous dialogue with other portions of ourselves, and to that extent this poetry reflects a process of give-and-take between psyche and self with which each of us is involved.

Others may not write poetry about it, but I believe that dreams, hunches, intuitions, and transcendent states of one kind or another are part of a natural process that allows us to keep in touch with the deepest elements of our being. The form or expression may vary, but the process itself cannot be stopped or stilled.

Jane Roberts
Elmira, N.Y.

CONTENTS

PART ONE

Getting Acquainted –
Questions and Answers

DIALOGUE ONE

Ah love
this stubborn mortal self,
determined, angry, outraged,
bleary, dizzy, loved,
holding its own in flesh and blood
amid the dazzling legislature
of the soul.

"There is no time or pain or death,"
the soul says,
and the mortal self shouts out,
"Ah, not for you. But I'm enclosed
in this body that decays.
At least it lives and loves
and laughs and cries for now.
Do you?

You keep immaculate distance,
yet through me you peek
into the time you say
is such a myth,
so my mortality must serve
your ends as well as mine.
I'd like to have less constant comment,
and if you can't say something nice
then shut up please.

And more:
Perfection isn't human
and here all creatures die.
The leaves fall downward, not up
for all your holy talk,
and I've never seen
one small corpse of a bird
pick itself up again and fly.

When I'm hurt, I don't need
your reminder, gentle or not,
that pain's an image in the mind.
Dreaming in this fragile stuff
of flesh and seasons since my birth,
I've coped
in the thickly webbed world of living thought
into which you plunged me, after all.
Amen."

The soul,
astounded, clears its throat
and waits, stunned,
for the mortal self to settle down.
"Oh, my, what metaphysical conceit.
You want bird corpses to fly,
(and in good light, I suppose,
not once or twice, but often enough
so you can be sure)
and the dead to speak, I've no doubt,
of their afterlife in the rosy glow.
Dear me. Now hear:

Your thoughts are like paintings
in your head,
only you fill them in with flesh,
frame them in the world of time
where each brushstroke comes alive,
and all the clouds really move
and all the houses have insides.
Even the tiniest smudge mark lives,
and ants teeter-totter
in the wiggly grass.

The living picture of the world
is painted by each and all.
Microbe, scholar, idiot, frog —
nail stuck in a sunny wall —
each to its own degree
stands up inside itself and shouts
and launches its image into space,
and each artist comes alive
in the world his thoughts have made.

Even the distance is built-in,
so that the corners really turn
and the people walk up and down
on paths they make as they go along.
Each birth and death happens in the mind
long before the church bells toll.
I try to give you good advice
but you twist around everything I say,
and do what you want to anyway."

DIALOGUE TWO

The Squirrel

Ah love
this mortal self who listens
and says, "Dear soul,
your marble words
go rolling through my bones,
from the mountains of my thoughts
down to my toes.
Your words are cold.
There is a language of the flesh
that I share with beast and bird,
a corporal anxiety
built into creaturehood
that you don't know.

And yet
just now I watched a squirrel.
He perched on a tiny branch
that thrashed in the winter wind,
and ate some seed.
You didn't see him afraid
of falling off,
or praying to *his* soul
for a better hold.
Perched atop his own mortality, he knew,
like some small furry god, secure
in a secret heaven of creaturehood
I've lost,
omnipotent in his own
processes.

Why should I envy him?
The squirrel can't write a poem.
He doesn't even know it's three o'clock.
Yesterday might as well not be
for all he can recall of it.
Yet he seems bristly
with a divinity I haven't got,
eternal and alive at once,
so ignorant
of his own mortality he'll live forever,
till his death, at least,
which won't impinge on him one bit, and so
has no reality.

How can he be so dumb
and live so well?"

The soul says, "Dear me,
I didn't realize
that you were in such a state.
Why don't you say
that you're the lowliest creature
in the universe,
and be done with it?
The trouble is that you see
but you don't look.

As for the squirrel,
he knows no duration.
Even if he lives a thousand years,
his minutes disappear
as if they never were.
His creature clarity is blessed
by instant cancellation
of his past
and where he is, is always.

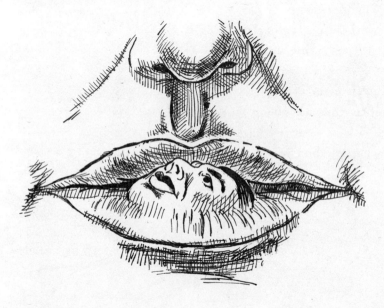

And more:
The squirrel's unknowing is the same
that allows you to speak your name,
though the cells within your lips
are ignorant of the alphabet
you learned in school.
As far as unknowing is concerned,
you don't even know how your body moves
its solid stuff from room to room.

On top of that, you leap
the branches of the months and weeks,
keep your footing, waking or asleep,
while swinging high in the jungle treetops
of your chirruping memories.
But all of this you ignore
in your blind envy of the squirrel.
He has his world and you have yours.

Your thoughts emerge
from the landscape of your mind
as easily as trees spring up outside.
Your intellect rides high, a moving
moon in that inner sky,
to illuminate the unknowing wisdom of the eye
that sees without knowing how
and does not question why."

DIALOGUE THREE

The Eyes

The mortal self
looks in the mirror
and says, "Dear soul,
ah love these spooky eyes,
as soft as flower petals
filled with moving skies,
tissues so alive and deep
and yet so small,
you could launch no craft inside
to explore
that depth that disappears,
but is so
miraculously devious.

These eyes
will congeal, and blind jelly
fill their shallow sockets
at my death,
perhaps two tablespoons full,
freshly harvested,
returned to the hidden
cabinets of earth;
unwiggling corneas stored unblinking
amid the long moonless gropings
and underground commotions
from which the occult spring
will again bring forth
its apport of flowers.

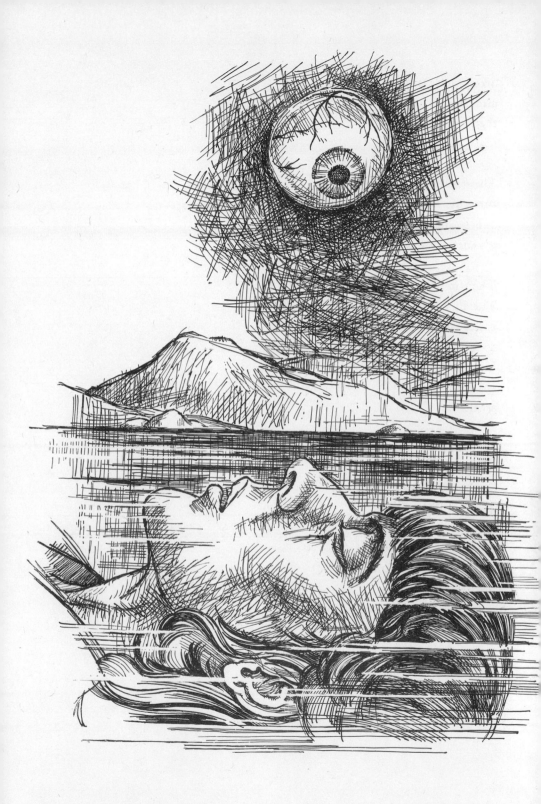

From that dark
underside of seeing,
then what vision
will you give me?"

The soul diplomatically
turns its head,
and waits till the mortal self
is more possessed.

Then it says, "Now wait.
The image you see in the looking glass
is fleeting and never fashioned
to last,
but your vision and what you are
is made of far more inscrutable
stuff.

In dreams
your eyelids are closed
as they will ever be,
yet you look
into worlds invisible,
that your physical eyes can't see.
You walk down unfamiliar streets
and meet strangers
you have known before,
yet all the while your body lies
quite safe and neat,
and never sets one foot
outside the door.

Asleep,
you forget the bureau and the chair,
and your address
is meaningless.
Your wardrobe might as well not be,
for all your love of propriety,
for while your body sprawls
in its wrinkled nightclothes,
you go abroad without a care
in attire never purchased in a store,
and sometimes
in no clothes at all.

Your body lies vacant-faced
like a doll on crisp white sheets,
alive but empty, don't you see?
You leave it, whole and intact,
to follow roads found on no map.
In dreams you use
the eyes of the soul,
that never need glasses
and can never be closed."

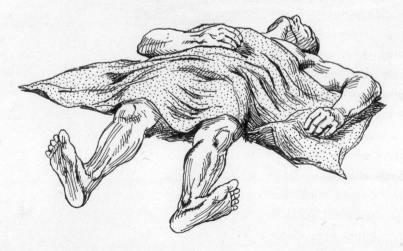

DIALOGUE FOUR

The Body's Warm Home

The mortal self shrugs and says,
"Dear soul,
how easily you speak
of life outside the flesh,
but, for me,
the body's warm home
is all I know,
and my tenancy
is brief at best.

It's true,
in dreams I've rushed
outside my bones
like smoke.
Once I breaststroked
through the clear night air
while my waiting
skeleton flashed white warning,
though the moonlight
was as thick as honey,

16

warm and glowing
in soft eddies past
my weightless arms.
Then a light blossomed
in my skull, and kept growing.
It included all I was,
filled my being,
and would have carried me
who knows how far
in that outside that has no boundaries
and no place to hide.

But I yelled and fell
through depth of god knows what,
that snuggled back
into this heated nest of skin and blood
that I call home.
It may be perilous, hung
between birth and death,
but this body's mine,
and dammit, loved."

The soul says fondly, "Now look.
Sulking won't help one bit,
and nowhere have I said
the body's wrong,
or suggested
that you leave it for good,
before its time.
I only said that you'll still live
even when your body's dead,
and I fail to see why that
should get you so upset.

Do you ever remember
a time when you weren't?
Do you ever remember
not being you?
You were yourself
before you were born
and put your present image on.

Before this life
you called the elements
from the four corners of the earth
to this one place and time.
They danced themselves into bone and blood,
adopting with corporal grace,
the form already spinning in your mind.
But as on earth all flowers die,
so you must return the borrowed stuff,
let loose the fabric, so the threads
can shape the living garments
of birds and beasts
as the living stitches of the molecules
flash back and forth through the centuries,
creating from the flesh of earth
patterns of death and birth.

So have you come and gone
through days and nights
in other forms,
looking out through other eyes
on familiar hands you called your own,
and wondering, when they were still,
how you could ever touch or will."

DIALOGUE FIVE

The Living Alphabet and the Geography of the Flesh

The mortal self frowns and says,
"Just the same,
I'm done with cowering.
I'll take my chances
with the squirrel.
I think that earth knows more
than it lets on,
and I suspect that the flesh
speaks a living alphabet,
in which the vowels and syllables
whisper themselves into molecules
and sing bodies instead of songs;
warm, woozy, dizzy sighs,
a language that comes alive
in skin and legs and bones and eyes.
So if death comes,
then I've been sung,
and done some singing on my own.

But love and hate
and peace and pain —
like dawn and dusk —
must have some place,
and to me at least it seems
you put earth down.

According to you, we sculpt
our lives out of our thoughts,
as if each one is a block
that comes to life and rests on top
of the one that came before,
so that we make the world we know
with living blocks, instead
of the wooden ones we piled
in stacks in school.

But the game is real to us
if a game is what it is,
and all your terms can't express
the vulnerability of the flesh.
So I prefer to hold my own
with the magic integrity of bone
that grows, or so it seems to me,
regardless of philosophy,
and the secret flow of my blood
is blessedly secure from all my thought,
rushing as it does
through caverns deep inside
the dark moorings of my heart."

The soul says, "Dear mortal self,
I don't know how
to set you straight,
your ideas are so far off.
Your thoughts are written in your skin.
Your blood is inaccessible, enclosed,
renewed from springs without openings;
yet its ancient eddies lap
against the hidden organ continents

that are moored so cleverly
in the geography
of your flesh.

The rivers of your blood flow
sweetly or darkly or fast or slow,
in sure accord
with the climate of your mind
that changes all the time.
The winds of hate
whip the blood into a dynamo
that lashes the floating edges
of the heart,
and sets in the breasts' soft hills
icy traps that catch
birds of love,
and won't let them go.

Your moods are changlings;
thoughts become feelings,
rising on tides of flesh,
their origin forgotten perhaps,
but written
in laughter or anger or love.

Tangled nerve ends tremble
in the treetops of your skull,
where, like squirrels, your thoughts climb
the brilliant branches
of your spine,
and memories buzz like a million bees
in hidden hives,
still stirring.

22

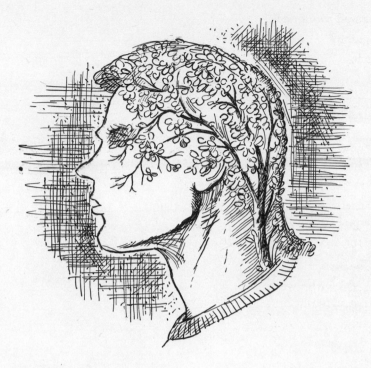

Your thoughts
are the hills and animals,
the birds and seasons
of inner worlds,
as you dwell in the universe outside."

DIALOGUE SIX

That Squirrel Again

The mortal self moans
and says, "Dear soul, enough.
I'm done,
exhausted, spent.
I've considered with awe
the giant responsibility
of my thought
until I'm afraid
I'll think myself to death,
and it seems safer
not to think at all.

Maybe I was better off
when I believed
there was some nice god,
and evil was the devil's fault.
At least I didn't have to feel
so concerned
when things went wrong.
And I've been remembering
that squirrel.

He doesn't think at all,
so it's obvious to me
that I think enough,
and probably too much
if the truth be known.

Will this thought get
the result I want?
Is it good or bad?
Am I projecting love or hate?
Oh, dear soul, save me
from such constant conscience.
If I were a squirrel,
I'd have fallen to my death,
getting my feet
all tangled up in my ideas.

So I'm done with worrying
and if today's mistakes
hit me in tomorrow's face,
that's just a chance
I'll have to take.
That squirrel's elegance
makes me ashamed.
If I moved with that same grace,
each of my thoughts would be
as secure as any
giant oak branch."
The soul thinks awhile
before it speaks.

Then it says, "Dear mortal self,
I'll try another analogy,
since you're so obsessed
with your squirrel.
You can leap as freely
through the treetops of your thoughts
as any squirrel scampers through an oak,
and, of course, you do.
I was only telling you
how things worked,
not suggesting you saw off
all your branches before you leap,
(so to speak).
That certainly makes
no sense at all.

I'll tell you once more:
Your thoughts rise from your mind
like the bushy branches of a tree.
They exist all at once,
rising and falling
in the winds of brain's morning
and evening.
Spread out all about you,
the bountiful expanse
of your thoughts' fruits
bloom and surround you
to sustain you,
even as the squirrel
has his seeds and nuts.

The fruits of your thoughts
are juicy and delicious
or sour and bitter,
and some are sweeter
than a pear or a peach.
You can pick and choose as you wish,
tasting and discarding,
but don't close your eyes
and try not to think,
or you'll find yourself
not only starving
but falling."

PART TWO

Soul and Self Meet
On a Rainy Weekend

The Paper and
Trips Through an Inner Garden

Ah love this mortal self
who finally says, "Dear soul,
I'm weary, and if you know so much,
then, wordless, let me touch
your knowledge
so that it overflows into my sense,
blooms in my molecules,
and forms an inner garden
I can walk into
on dark days."

The soul smiles and says,
"It's already there.
I thought you'd never ask."
And exasperated,
the mortal self cries out,
"Then where? In what direction?
In this maze of inner verbiage,
where's the path
and more,
why is it hidden, not open?
If there's a garden,
why hide the gate?"

The soul momentarily withdraws
and tries again. "Now hear.
Be quiet if you can,
just for a change.
Sometimes I think
you don't hear a thing I say.
Don't you ever play?
You're so ponderous
that my humor falls
on deaf ears.

You ask questions just to ask,
then race through the answers
just to see
where you disagree.
I can play that game as well as you.
But if you'd just be still
and playfully pretend
you didn't care,
and give up your questions for a while,
you'd find
answers opening up inside your head."

The mortal self drums its fingers
and says,
"All right. I'm waiting,"
and pours a cup of tea
and lights a cigarette.
"Don't wait," the soul sighs,
"just be. Feel your being opening
like flowers in the morning.
Know your toes,
merry in their sockets,
nuzzling the floor;
the living pressure of your skin
breathing out and in
with each gentle nudge of air.
Feel your soft eyes,
as innocent and wild
as any animal's,
looking out into the universe
with ancient knowing
yet uncalculating grace."

So the soul speaks,
slyly, softly,
until the mortal self
finally
lets down its guard.
Then it says,
"Open your eyes.
The garden grows all about you
where it was all the time.
But go ahead, say something.
I can tell
that you're surprised."

And the mortal self shouts out,
"Why, everything's living —
I mean, the couch and chair
are like flowered creatures,
placid but aware — and as I look,
I see them pulsing,
changing in the light
as if talking back
or lapping up
spoonfuls of the air.
And the oak table is
still filled
with memories of the tree it was,
and the sound of birds
rises out of it, chirruping,
and the chattering of squirrels;
and it's alive, solid, and moving
all at once.
I can reach my hand down through the wood
and touch an April branch.

But wait —
I see a piece of paper
outside the window
in the street.
Oh watch it move,
surfing in the waves of air,
just waiting for the highest surge
and jumping in,
or leaping up the shining hills of space
and flying down
the valley side.
It lands by a blue, dark shadow
that isn't flat at all,
but a smooth, cool, and secret
creature brought to life
by the moment's
wind and light.
Oh, shadow, brilliant
and dark at once,
how dear you are in this
bright instant
of the universe.
Now, oh now the paper moves,
I swear by its own accord!
It wants
to feel the breeze beneath it push
and thrills to give its own response.

Oh watch it go,
skimming like a floppy butterfly,
wings flapping,
touching but not quite touching

the walk
and lifted up again,
dizzy, delirious,
its own sounds crackling
against its insides,
and the air rubbing
upon its edges
with a muted twang.
If that paper moves again,
I think I'll die.
I swear I can't look
any longer
or I'll take leave
of all my sense."

The soul says,
"You saw me.
I was the paper
and yet the paper was itself.
You saw what the paper was
when you forgot
how paper should behave.
Now close your eyes.
What do you see?"
The mortal self hesitates
and says, "I'm scared.
The paper was outside
and my eyes were open.
I could have closed them
if I wanted,
and the paper would
have disappeared.

But wait. I see a tree.
It's real — I mean, natural —
yet made of jeweled colors
that sing, ring
like a million different bells,
all melodious.
And these . . . sounds twirl, solidify,
forming mesh-like shapes that dance
themselves into visibility
and thicken into fruit."

The mortal self can barely speak.
It cries, "Look,
the fruit dances about the tree,
those tinted vowels or sounding hues,
in all stages of becoming —
some only transparent colors
hanging in the air,
others shiny, round, and solid.
Oh, I see some unforming again,
dropping their long, blue sighs
into the long-toned ground."

The mortal soul cries out
and says, "Dear soul,
where does the tree exist?
What glowing world is this
behind my closed eyelids?
If I insist
on opening my eyes,
will it all vanish?
Or is the tree always there,
its sounds spinning into color,

conjuring solidity and form
out of the gracious,
transparent air?

Dear soul, am I awake
and reasoning?"
The soul, smiling, answers,
"Yes, you are,"
and the mortal self replies,
"Then the oddest thing is happening.
I seem to stand at the open window,
looking down
at the apple tree in the yard out back.
The air is heavy as water,
only thicker
and I can stir it with my hand.
It's soft as jelly, clear, and look —
falling from my fingertips,
it forms kaleidoscopes
of jelly cubes.

Everything that I can see —
sky, ground, trees —
is filled with these
clumps of color,
each apart and glowing,
yet spilling one into the other
like magic gelatin,
shaking and alive with light.
I shove my hand into that shining stuff
and my arm's weightless,

as if
the air forms a liquid shelf,
and my arm floats in it
like a long
semisolid fish.

The currents eddy outward
at my touch,
stirring the branches of the tree,
and I can see those same ripples move,
ascending to the sky,
nuzzling the clumps of cloud above
and go waking through the universe.
Good god!

And the tree is rooted
not only to the ground,
which is also fluid,
but all its edges and smallest twigs
emerge from space,
growing as much into the tree
as out of it,
newly
solidifying into focus
from this primeval
yet freshly harvested jellied air."

The mortal self laughs
and poises full-length
on the dream windowsill.
"If I let go, I won't fall,
only float in slow motion
from here to there,
through the yielding ground

which is also rising and falling,
transparent,
growing and ungrowing.
I could
drift through it forever
and never move.

But what happened?
Suddenly the air is thin again.
Its hills and curves
and cubed kaleidoscopes are gone.
My hand is empty,
and only moments ago it was filled
with sparkling miniature
jelly molds of space.
Dear soul!"

Aftermath and
Arguments on a Friday Afternoon

The mortal self opens its eyes and says,
"It's over, and I'm relieved.
It's scary to feel so good, so free,
and something holds me back
so that I want to cry
myself to death
in the face of such ecstasy.
Joy and panic hold me equally,
as if such a gift must have its price,
and I want to know just what it is.

We have our ancient fables.
I know they're superstitious,
yet if you sell your soul to the devil,
you know the terms
and you haven't got much to say
when he collects —
and not much left, anyway —
but what price do we pay
for the gifts of the gods?
Nobody knows.
Are they given for nothing?
Exultation and madness spring
alike from visions
beyond imagining.

So I pause before I leap,
heart swollen with wonder,
and while I stand at such
a precipice,
I look over my left shoulder.
I've heard
that the gods' gifts were fruits
that turned to poison —
blessed, delicious, but oh,
treacherous and habit-forming,
so that earthly varieties
tasted forever afterward
like ashes.

I don't know why gods and devils
came to mind.
I don't believe in either,
and they'd both be strange to me.
I've never read a book
on a god's psychology.
Motives quite natural to them
might seem
insane or inconceivable to me,
and animals, alien to some degree,
at least are visible.

Is it safe to feel so good,
or does it make the gods jealous?
Wouldn't it be smarter, slyer
for me to beat my chest
and pretend to pay a price
in case I can't afford the cost?"

The soul walks about the room
and begins to dust the furniture,
bustling about,
while the mortal self just stands,
nonplussed. It says,
"What are you doing? Have you gone mad?
Here I am, nearly scared to death,
and you're dusting the table
and making the bed."

The soul, unperturbed,
shrugs, and works on.
Then it says,
"I suggest you buy a whip
and a coat of nails,
and take a bath in tar and ash,
and beat yourself twice a day.
It seems you want to, anyway."

The mortal self shouts back,
"Will you please give me
that dustcloth?
Souls aren't supposed to work at all.
Besides, you make me nervous,
and you look so much like me
that I get confused."

The soul replies,
"You certainly do.
Besides, this is a quiet interlude
meant to calm you down.
I'm trying to prove
that I'm a dependable,
daily sort of soul,
quite equipped to help you function
in the normal world
and no one to be frightened of
at all.
At least my polishing of the furniture
makes you forget
that nonsense about devils and such.
Now, if you don't mind,
please hand me the wax."

"Stop that,"
  cries the mortal self.
"I don't trust you one bit.
  You're planning something, I can tell,
  but at least
  you're visible."

  The soul says dryly,
"Like the animals?
  See, you gave yourself away.
  But more, you're seeing what you want to see
  and that has little to do with me,
  but by all means,
  trust your own perceptions."
The soul turns around and coughs,
  and conceals a smile
  while pretending to shake out
  the dustcloth.

"Then what can I trust?"
  cries the mortal self.
"If I can't trust perceptions,
  there's damn little left."

The soul says,
"Trust your perceptions
as perceptions.
They're pictures of the world
seen from one direction,
packaged and assembled
by the nerves and brain,
a gift box for the senses in which
jigsaw images
appear to hand and eye,
a do-it-yourself kit
of creation,
sent to the self
in the world of time.

The package is so attractive
it takes all of your attention,
but such a gift is made
to make you question:
Who is the giver
and who left the mail?
You can at least
examine the contents and wonder:
Are there other boxes
beside the one you hold in your hand?"

The mortal self stops dead and says,
"Then I'm not seeing you at all?
I'm imagining this whole thing.
I don't know who's more inventive,
you or me."
The soul replies

"You're seeing through the package.
Very good.
The wrappings are quite transparent,
once you learn to see and not just look.
I'm as real as you are,
or you're as real as me,
but there are journeys ahead for us,
and we may as well
get started now."

Ah love this mortal self
who shrinks
back against the couch
and says, "Oh, no, not me.
No more trips inside my head
to places nobody else can find.
Why don't you mind
your own business like any other soul?
You go your way
and I'll go mine."

The soul just laughs and laughs,
then finally says,
"Dear mortal self,
your suggestion is hilarious,
like trying to cut
the sky in half.
No body or soul
has that kind of scissors.
You can't cut a hole in the sky,
much less divide it,
it won't break up into pieces.
So you can't cut your soul
out of your heart
even if you were silly enough
to try it."

Celebration of the Squirrels and
Double Worlds

Ah smile at this mortal self
who sits eating breakfast toast.
It looks out the window
at the trees and yard below
and suddenly shouts out,
"Oh, look, look, look;
two — no, three — squirrels
go skimming
through the oak tree outside.

But wait, another leaps
from the peaked roof next door
and slides down the invisible air,
bushy tail flying.
He leaps to those tiny twigs —
they'll never hold — but they do!
Wham! He lands on them,
going how many miles an hour,
and they go twanging back and forth
as he jumps off.

And there go more;
three squirrels chasing each other
through the gaps of air.
That one slid five feet straight
down to the trunk, then leapt
six to another quaking branch —

furry gods at play again —
and listen
to the jay's squawking in the swirls
of sky above where I can't see.

The whole space
between this house and the next
is so alive
it makes me dizzy.
Oh, the squirrels are gone.

Now a lone pigeon sits on the chimney top,
like me,
climbing to the top of myself and looking out.
What does he see,
wings so easily folded,
so magnificently physical
that he seems to carry
creaturehood out of its degree;
so perfect
in his secure unknowing ease?

Oh, if this day
teaches me anything,
let me learn
the squirrel's and the pigeon's
trusting unconcern,
and approach that grace
that moves them safely
through the shining
unknowing knowledge of their way."

The mortal self
pours a cup of coffee
and says,
"I write a poem
and trust it will be done
once it's begun,
and feel that swift acceleration,
as if I move faster than bird or squirrel,
as you say, through the shaking
forests of my mind,
so that sometimes I just catch glimpses

of where I've been.
A power fills me up and supports me
that I trust.
Though I grow light-headed
I never look down, but feel
the beckoning of still higher perches,
take rest in unsuspected
sudden places,
then leap to tiny rocking concepts
that sway like twigs
way above the universe,
and slide down so fast
I nearly bunk my head;
and doing this, I feel
more alive than any squirrel.

And yet,
returning I pause
and lose my bearing,
and where my body is concerned,
I forget
that brilliant coordination
that my mind has learned.
I keep
trying to make corrections,
yet all the while I know
the answer is in not trying
to know what I must know.

The squirrels' celebration
of the morning
has a meaning that I'm meant to see,

and I wonder if they appeared
out of their own intent,
or yours, or mine, or both,
or if in some shining altogether
we joined,
and knowing and unknowing, danced
through dimensions I can barely glimpse,
that are as close
as my eyes and hands."

The mortal self frowns
and says,
"It seems
that those squirrels come
like apports
from another world
just when
I need them most,
and it makes me curious
about something else.
Do the living appear to the dead,
as they say the dead do
to the living,
and as easily as those squirrels
appeared to me,
seemingly out of nowhere;
or isn't there any correlation?

Yet those squirrels and pigeons
are as miraculous
as any vision.
A ghost could understand my talk —
at least I suppose he would —
while the solid squirrel,
so bristly and alive
in this real world
would chatter in his own language
and not hear a thing I say.

So nature
is as alien in its way
as ghosts or apparitions,
and the squirrels as magical
as that tree I saw whose sounds
spun themselves
into fruit.
For all I know, perhaps
the jay's noisy squawks
drop into the air
in glimmering forms and shapes
right now, that I don't see
but only hear.
How strange, and who knows
where this is leading to?"

"It isn't leading anywhere,"
  the soul says.
"That's the point.
  The alien and the natural are one,
  the squirrels and visions,
  rising in the sudden world,
  as the tree was, that splendidly
  emerged within your head.
  You saw each when you wanted to,
  and both exist at once."

"But —
  real squirrels don't scramble
  down imaginary trees,"
  the mortal self says,
  annoyed at feeling some relief
  as it thinks of this,
"And invisible squirrels don't play
  in that real oak tree."

  The soul smiles.
"You wouldn't see them
  if they did."

  The mortal self shakes its head
  and says, "Oh, come now,
  you don't mean
  ghost squirrels?"

"Who said ghosts?"
  the soul replies,

"Real squirrels, though not physical
clamping padded paws in wood and bark
and sliding through air's open gaps,
living but invisible,
still there
though their bodies may have died
a year ago at Christmastide.

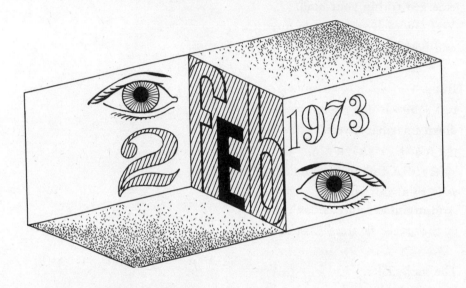

The worlds are merged
and overlapped,
and each moves through the other,
so that even standing still
you move through worlds invisible.
February the second,
nineteen seventy-three
is a place in that other space
that you can visit any time.
It appears in its own way,
and the road's not hard to find.

For each world is a map
of its counterpart,
and time grows like a mountain
from the foothills of the heart.
Walk up its slopes to the top,
and all the time you've known
is spread
out before you, sparkling;
and if, once there,
you close your eyes,
then north and south and east and west
disappear and in their place
the four corners of the soul are there.

So amuse yourself and pluck
the wild flowers that grow
from the rich slopes
of your heart.
Let us stand at the top and feel
both worlds merge into ourselves.
Let us, using our double vision,
travel two worlds in one,
and form
a single-double song
that splashes out in ripples
of thought and blood
that eddy, wrinkle, and wake
through the double skies
of our single universe, and break
into rainbow vowels that sing
soft lullabies
that fall as light
in both our worlds."

Single-Double Worlds, the Rain Creature, and the Light

The mortal self
sometime later says,
"That light, striking,
what did it touch
and was it real?
Just now I stood
by the open kitchen window,
looking down again at the rainy street.
Only now it's dark.
I've written all day long
and done my chores
and company is coming
so my mind was blank.

Yet I was caught, transfixed.
The raindrops fell
in thousands of separate sparkling dots
into a puddle far below,
and as I watched
the puddle rose up, thickened
into prickly tissue like an air-filled lung
or porcupine of light,
with the raindrops growing out of it
as much as in.

It drank the reflections
from the passing car headlights,
and they rushed into it blindly
till it was so full it pulsed —
a shining, fluid, living thing.
The rain slid off its smooth, liquid skin
and there stood a creature so mobile —
each part moving and alive, sliding, shimmering —
that I closed my eyes.

I opened them instantly.
The creature'd flattened out again,
but just began to rise
when everything I saw
went through my soul.
Our worlds merged and I cried out;
and as I did, a soft sudden
circle of light appeared,
right in front of me,
well-defined, between the refrigerator
and the stove.

It startled me so
that I leapt back —
a softly glowing circle
waist-high in the air
to above my head;
not a ball of fire but a silent,
round, unmoving light,
and no illumination spread
outward from its edges,
so the rest of the room
was still dark.

Lightning, of course,
but there was no beam of light
inside the room or without
from which it came.

It hung in the air
like a sudden flat sunflower,
larger than life,
minus seeds and stem.
An omen?
The light you spoke of
that would unite our double-
single worlds, appearing
in my universe from yours?
Whatever its cause or origin,
I felt it appeared for a reason
and I'd like to know
what that reason is.

I know the puddle was natural,
and in this world, flat;
while with other vision
I saw its counterpart
rise up, all shining,
and nearly walk.
But if that light came
from the world I know
then I have to admit
I don't know how.

But, dear soul,
I'm afraid I can't wait
for your reply just now.
I hear my company,
and I'm glad to just sit and chat
this stormy night,
while that rainy wind blows."

The Fetus

The next morning the soul says,
"You see, when self and soul
move as one,
they easily surpass your plucky squirrel.
In the past, you saw two worlds,
one a time of seasons, pain, and death,
in which you lived
housed in flesh;
and another distant one
from which the soul sent messages,
cheering you on from the sidelines,
but not participating
as you did.
You saw me as aloof, serene, and dead
to all the things that meant
so much to you,
so you felt cut off."

"Wait — the phone —"
the mortal self says.
It speaks awhile and then returns.
"Dear soul,
talk about your double worlds!
Well, a friend just called
from out of town.

She's pregnant three months
and going to abort.
It's all quite legal,
but what about the fetus, journeying
from that other universe to this?
It'll never land alive here,
that's for sure,
or stand up on its own feet
to investigate the world
it was heading for.

If the fetus is a tiny vehicle,
and a consciousness leaps in,
traveling through dimensions of space and tissue
in ways we can barely understand
to emerge finally through
the black hole of the womb
into events and time,
then what happens
when the vehicle's misshapen,
or encounters enemies
at this end?"

The soul says, "Dear friend,
you, too, made such voyages.
The seeds fly out of the flowers,
riding the wind.

Some land
in fertile soil at once.
Others fall on rock
and try again.

So the fetus is a cocoon
spun in the web
of time and blood,
so cunningly attuned
to your world and mine
that each tissue is alive,
trembling.
The fetus is hung
like a cradle, then,
and the self enters in
like a tiny king
when all is prepared
and everything is in readiness,
and the earth provides its best —
a new, living, private
kingdom of the flesh.

And the fetus is a nest hung
in the fibrous branches
of the tree of life,
dangling out

between the centuries,
protected,
snug for the moment.
Unfilled, it falls back
into the unknown knowing
that gave it form;
and some self won't waken
in the world of the hours
but lives, just as before,
in worlds of its own,
or waits
for a better flight."

PART THREE

Death of a Cat, Senility, and Joy

The mortal self says, "Dear soul,
I thought I'd ask you about problems
as they came up for a while,
since we're getting along so well,
but today I can hardly
write or speak
and ideas of inner gardens
are furthest from my mind.
Let me wash my face
and wipe my eyes
and I'll begin."

A Lyric to Rooney

"Dear soul,
our cat Rooney died today,
February 5, 1973,
of god knows what disease.
We buried him in the garden
and marked the spot
with one rock,
so let whoever or whatever there is
treat him gently.
At least we did.
The earth received him
without a murmur.
I wrapped him in our best tablecloth
since he is to be the worms' dinner,
but oh, I trust he knew the terms,
and one
who acquiesces to the sun
has no fear of worms.
In some way that cat triumphed,
coming and going
unperturbed.

When people die
they're dressed and pampered
and lie in state,
primped-up and powdered
so they look alive,
their corpses hidden
beneath Sunday clothes,
the folds and frills arranged
so that no naked inch

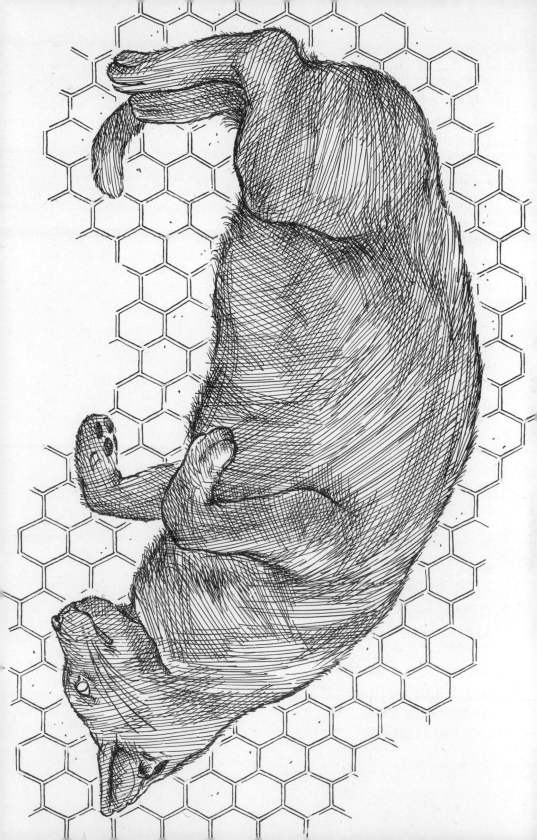

of death-caked skin shows,
only the face fuzzy with rouge
and the talcumed smooth hands.
The rigid body beneath
might as well not be
for all we can see of it,
as if one look at that truth
would close our eyes
forever too.

But my cat's still warm body lay
heavier than it ever was,
undisguised,
its death still happening,
black fur thick and deep,
yet alive, but quieting
like a dying blanket
flat against its silent back.

There was no breath,
yet the eyes opened
and we leapt back,
but the eyes were that blind jelly,
pupils stuck in it
and the creature had left its flesh.
The form was stiffening
into a final sculpture
of the cat
in which life had been.
Yet from that utter rigidity
and even in it, there was motion sensed,
disquieting but sure,

of matter loosening
and a different kind of freedom
rushing slowly in.

We buried Rooney,
as I said, in the yard,
and again there was that
strange life-in-death
not sensed at funerals,
in which the integrity of death
shone with its own
pure arithmetic — subtraction
turning into addition
in the rich calculus
of earth.

I cried;
yet in the flow of my tears,
felt the motion of my being
and knew
that it moves us through death,
which is another expression of ourselves,
or a process
through which our being passes.

I felt the connection
between that fetus
I mentioned earlier — scrawny;
nothingness fashioning
a skeleton, still unfleshed —

and Rooney unbecoming a cat,
his corpse falling back,
its flesh disappearing
as mysteriously
as it came.

Yet I shouted out in joy
at my brilliant creaturehood
and felt desire
run out of my toes.
But just the same, I defy
any god to cast a stone at us,
or send down plagues
or pestilence or floods
and I'd be bound to ask
'What's new?'
They're all part and parcel
of our creaturehood,
so any judgment is ours
as far as I'm concerned.

I think the answers
are in our flesh,
all bound up in the world we know —
where we're going and where we've been
are all contained in this Now,
written in sun and winter,
rain and snow,
hills and valleys and afternoons
that one by one
disappear
into dusk."

The soul replies,
"Dear mortal self,
death is living within you now,
even as in death, there's life.
Your being embraces both,
and rises alike from each.
Let your life grace
all crannies of your flesh,
joyfully perceiving its richness
through the living mirror
of your uniqueness,
in which forever your own life shines
and no other."

The mortal self says,
"Yeah, but what about my cat?
In a world of wars and terror
I'm almost embarrassed
to speak of that,
a minor household tragedy,
and who cares?

Yet I stubbornly insist
that if a cat's death doesn't matter,
then there's no meaning
anywhere.

I don't expect to see that cat's ghost
chasing birds in the yard come spring,
though today I looked,
feeling like an ass, as I came up the stair.
But I remember my old remark,
'here bird corpses don't fly,'
and dead cats don't race
to their plates at dinnertime;
not that Rooney raced, he ambled,
big and fat and gentle,
but best I don't
go into that.

As I write, my other cat
Willy's sitting in my lap.
He's lonesome, I suppose.
Anyway he's been
following me around all day.
But what part do we play
in the life of animals?

We first saw Rooney
one frosty February day.
He was starving, cold, and scrawny,
his fur ice-matted and clammy.
We threw fresh food
down to him in the yard,

yet he was so scared
that he wouldn't eat
till we were gone.

I saw him, small and angry,
trying to bite through
the icy ball that surrounded
the freezing food.
Still he wouldn't come near us,
much less into the house,
and though we moved the food
closer to the door each time,
it was June
before he stepped suspiciously
into the hall.

We tempted him, then.
He didn't want to come.
Was he somehow
supposed to die that winter,
wild, free, but starving
out in the snow? Just sleep
himself to death
in a night of February ice?

His wild gut cry
used to startle neighbors at midnight,
and they'd come out, yelling
in their nightclothes,
to find Rooney
in blood and gory battle

with another tom, both bristling,
eyes like miniature flashlights
brighter than any
you'd ever buy in a store.

We had him fixed.
He grew fat and seemed content
but opulent,
sagging somehow,
and he never played
but slept all day,
yellow eyes wandering in their luster.

Yet still
he vanished when anybody came
and with us he was always hesitant,
not a friend but a thing between.
He'd rather have been an enemy,
fighting what he didn't understand.

So, did we betray him
with our sympathy?
Or was our sympathy just fear?
We took him in, or I did,
thinking that if we could save that cat
from death and cold,
we'd saved everything.
And he was always sick.
We kept him from his death too long
and I wish I'd let him die
as he was going to,
as the ferocious

yet acquiescent,
proud and wild creature,
asking nothing of the elements,
but yowling out
his yellow-eyed dissent.

He might have lived
without our food,
scrounging around the neighborhood,
and dying in one last
March battle,
seasons later,
while the spring moon's
yellow eyes, brighter than his,
at last enclosed him.

Instead he died on the tiled
bathroom heated floor,
with no hole to nuzzle in; no ground.
So perhaps wild things should be left wild,
and maybe the wildness in us
is some pure, seeming savagery
in which greater wisdom rides
than we suppose,
and in trying to be so spiritual
we've overlooked
an omnipotence of creaturehood
that's in us all the while.
So though it may not sound logical,
I think that Rooney's finally free.

And more: I've watched the senile
sitting up with their bibs

tied beneath their chins,
force-fed, with hands as inert
as sick cat paws, dangling;
many there in nursing homes because
they rushed through suburban backyards
at midnight, rattling garbage cans,
or bungled their bleary way in front of cars
and worried their relatives.
So they're tranquilized.
But even then
some brass-yellow boldness leaps up
till they're strapped down.

My husband's father was such a one,
and while I said,
'Nothing can be done,'
some part of me yearned to turn him loose,
holy and wild with his burning creaturehood,
to make what peace
with earth he could.
So let him run, bitterly or with childish glee
through winter woods in his hospital clothes,
or waving his arms like a crazy tree, stop traffic,
falling in his living tracks
like an animal felled cleanly;
but he died like the cat
in more
humane surroundings.

Yet senile
the old man was kinder
than he had ever been before.
He seemed to open like a flower
buds of love

that had been closed,
and he dozed
like an animal in the sun,
lounging
upon some gracious inner
couch of being
that we
could only sense.
So perhaps we didn't harm
him or the cat after all.

My father, a much younger man,
went after a bout of drink, I suspect
alive into his death
so to speak, just last year.
I wouldn't be surprised if
he was too drunk to know
that he wasn't still alive,
and I can see him reeling gloriously
into that afterlife,
gradually gaining
sobriety by degrees.
And I assume he chose that way,
going fast and fortified
and certainly not singing hymns,
and to that I'd like to say
Amen.

My mother lived and died in pain,
and for years her terror
tiptoed through the corners
and corridors of my brain,

till my joys turned into cowards,
afraid to show their faces,
hiding behind the memory of a fear
they couldn't understand.

But each woman and man alive
must stand up inside themselves
one day and shout,
'I turn toward life, and accept
those conditions of the earth
into which I was once born, unknowing,'
and in so doing, find
a second birth of consciousness,
accepting its marriage
with the flesh
and I'd like to go on record
as taking just that stand."

The soul smiles and says, politely,
"Dear mortal self, accept
my condolences
on the, uh, death of your cat,
but his consciousness
flew out of his skin
before the body died
and the pain wasn't connected
to a living brain,
but fell apart
into separate tissue deaths
that smoothly slide
into different form,

and feel their oneness breaking down
without alarm,
joyful
in acquiescence.

And each being
retains its memory,
as each atom holds within itself
the imprint of the star
from which it came.

Rooney in a way
will wander that backyard,
at least for a while,
his consciousness leaping out
in a thousand eyes
from bush and leaf and tree,
pursuing his enemies

and pouncing as before,
but through wind and gusts
of snow
instead of with his paws.
He doesn't know that he is dead.
He's changed his way of life instead,
responding now in different ways
than his cathood would allow."

PART FOUR

Body, Soul, World

Body

Ah sigh
for this bemused mortal self,
still unsure
where body and soul
begin or end,
trying to ally itself
with whichever one
might prove to be
the most powerful friend.
It sits writing again,
looking out the window
at the oak and house and street.
The surviving cat,
more pampered now than it ever was,
meows, and the mortal self
springs up with a gasp of surprise
and says:

"Look at that cat,
how solid and packed
its body is,
and when I touched Rooney
he was thick and real in space too,
even dead;
but I've never thought of my flesh
like an object in a room
with mass and weight
to be seen by others like a chair.
Right now I feel flat,
not in the world, but

looking out at it as if it's stretched
in front of me,
ending sideways at my vision;
and nothing exists behind my back
where I can't see,
no room or furniture.

Maybe I've lost touch
with my organism
and become, in the oddest way,
detached.
Strange if thoughts
of a dead cat's body
brought me back.
I see I've felt
more invisible than visible,
and for all my talk
I feared
identification with my flesh.
So it occurs to me that we hide
our living bodies in our clothes
and not just the finished ones
at funerals.

My body flattened out
into an idea,
and I tried to make it
as mental as I could.
I've seen my image in the glass
and I felt like that,
a flat reflection on a flat surface,
not round or thick,
with nothing between my chest
and back but space.

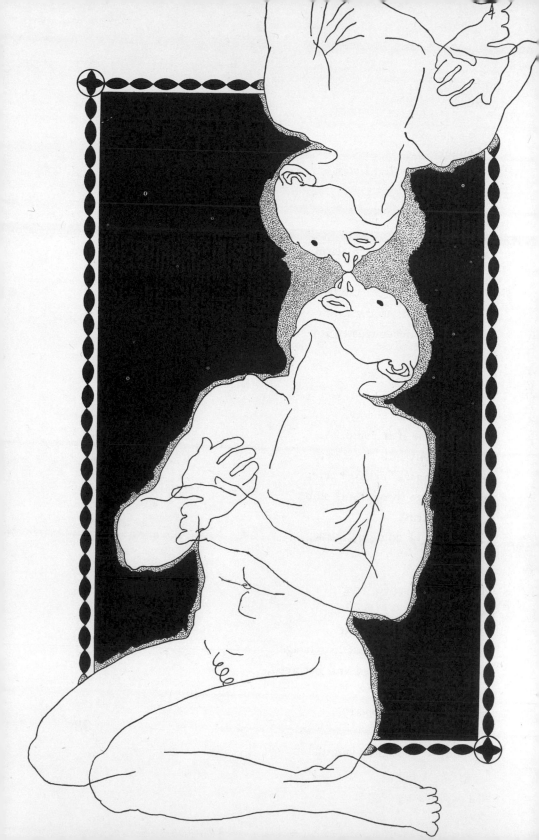

So I felt
unfilled.

I thought
that the less physical I was,
the less
vulnerable I'd become.
Each smallest pain
flashed through me with alarm,
reminding me
of the body's unpredictability.
It could hurt me at any time
and I guess I never trusted it
but feared
it would lose me in its
creaturehood.
I considered it an enemy,
out to get me if it could.
I can look out into the street
to see if danger's lurking there,
but I can't see through my skin
so I didn't trust
what might be going on inside.

My mind, detached, apart,
felt lonely,
yearning for its other part,
and my body yelled out its outrage
to be thus disinherited and betrayed,
and so we only met
opaquely through poetry,
where I could keep
my body at thought's length.

I'd say Hello,
but I'm afraid that it might
not answer back,
and I really didn't think
it had a part to play
in these dialogues.
With you on one side
and my body on the other,
where the hell do I belong?

What did I say just yesterday
about a second birth in flesh?
I guess I didn't realize even then
just what I'd done, or what I meant.
Now that I think of it, I know
that others in their own way
do the same damn thing.

We try to hide
our cocky flesh in clothes
and pretend that we're just minds
strutting about in thin air,
except perhaps when we're very young
and the body's still the splendid thing
we know it is, before we're told
that it's somehow wrong."

Ah love this mortal self
who grins then craftily and says,
"Dear soul, just how old are you anyhow?
Or aren't I supposed to ask?
You're older than my body, I suppose,
so you must have some kind of stamina
belonging to each of us that I can use."

The You-ness of the Universe

The soul smiles
even more craftily, and replies,
"I'm all of your ages: twelve and thirty
and seventy-two, all together
in one invisible package,
from which you leap
like a jack-in-the-box
into the world of time.

I'm the you
from which your you-ness
constantly appears.
I'm the you-ness of the universe,
that part of All That Is
that wakens to Itself as you,
and each day joyfully
creates your mind and image,
down to your smallest molecules,
rising from unimaginable love
into the infinite tender specifics
from which
your you-ness comes.

I'm that part
of your ever emerging
you-ness,
springing into expression,
that part of All That Is that follows you
through all of your creations
and sensations,
that part of the source from which

you form your world and make your image,
for you and the source are one.
It supports
your you-ness even through your deaths
of forms and holds it
ever inviolate.

I've always known myself as you
and sung your you-ness into being,
and I dance now
through the magic of your knees and ankles
in the splendor of your secret morning,
dazzled and alive and knowing
through the buzzing warmth of your body,
formed by you from
the you-richness of God's being.

Transubstantiation —
the spirit made flesh,
becoming tissue in each moment,
drawn according to your thoughts and wishes
freshly out of the invisible you-forming mind.
The body *is* you,
as you constantly transform yourself into living
your you-ness in earth form.

The wind blows in all directions.
Its agility astounds
the corners of the world.
It rushes through your backyard,
whipping the weeds into waves of motion,
so the breath of your you-ness
rushes through your blood and bone,
moves joyfully
with instant elation,
its agility alive
in the tiniest leap of your hand.
Your body is swirling,
packed full of flesh,
filled with motion unending
until its death.

You're not locked into mortality.
You flow through it,
your you-ness bursting newly
in space and time.

You constantly ripple
into swirls of tissue
that then move through the air,
as if the wind suddenly solidified
and like your rain creature, came alive,
and even this poem
is physical.

Your fingers don't understand
the words they write,
yet their motions follow your will
so perfectly that the words appear
like messages

from another world
emerging in pen and ink upon the page —
and all of this because
the living nerves move so swiftly back and forth,
carrying signals that have nothing to do
with books or words,
but with miracles of flesh,
themselves
biological vowels,
singing songs that keep
your bowels and heart alive.

And when you speak the words aloud,
your voice itself rides
on rhythms of blood and breath
so deep and sure
that your sentences
are only surface symbols
carrying messages
quite apart from what they say,
for the sounds emerge
from magical gut utterances in which
yellow-eyed cells shout out in vowels,
and rush into the transparent air
and speak, dear self, within your words,
consonants unheard
from a language in which
vocabulary springs
from open tissue mouths.

You laugh with joy
now as you write
and hear that laugh!

What noises unite and rise
on lifts of feeling,
pushing your lips apart,
and all the little wrinkles
slide up, crackling in sounds
that you can't hear
just behind your moving skin
which gives
on the slippery undersides,
so ripples spread their glowing paths
up to the tiny waving
lashes of your eyes.
How strange that I
should have to tell you this.
Do you still think
that I'm trying to put the body down?"

Ah laugh and cry with this mortal self
who says,
"I wish you'd tell my sinuses.
They bother me all the while,
but I certainly feel more physical
and I'll say one thing,
you certainly know how to make me smile."

The soul inclines its head and says,
"No tree drives itself crazy
trying to discover where
its bark begins or ends,
or at what precise point its roots
disappear into the ground,
or tries to discriminate
between its flowers, leaves, and fruits.

It has more sense,
and grows out through space
one graceful inch at a time,
without stopping to check
its direction at every turn.
And if you left yourself alone,
your body would grow as merrily
as any tree.

106

If you let yourself be,
you wouldn't have any trouble
with your sinuses.
And now it's my turn to say
Amen."

The mortal self grins and says,
"Going back to what you said
a few moments ago,
where does the world I know begin?
Can I catch it happening,
and see objects being born?"

The soul replies,
"Dear mortal self,
the world of facts
and squirrels and cats
begins where consciousness
connects with flesh
and comes alive in the world of sense
where beliefs all turn into events,
emerging from realms invisible
into which they will return again.

The universe knows who you are
and recognizes each
microbe and fish and frog
and smallest corner of the world
as a portion of itself
flowering into actuality."

107

The soul pauses and says,
"Dear mortal self,
feel your living leaping
alive anew in each moment.
Live in the starry framework
of dawn and evening,
content to be carried
by the rhythms of your being,
expressing freely
the miracles of feeling
that flow and eddy
through the ever changing
fields of your flesh."

PART FIVE

Feelings and
Inner and Outer Landscapes

Another Phone Call

Ah sigh for this mortal self who says,
"The phone. Sorry, dear soul,
I'll be right back,"
and on returning, writes,
"Another woman called.
She just lost her job and wanted me to talk,
so I said yes, and now I'm mad.
'Why bother me?' I thought,
while I felt that I should help,
so I banged the bed
with my badminton racket
as hard as I could,
wanting to yell,
'World, get off my back!'

How come this rage?
'Express your feelings' —
that's easy enough for you to say.
You probably feel good
all of the time, while I
know hate is buried like a bone somewhere
in a hole hidden behind my mind
and I'm afraid I'll dig it up unwittingly
if I start feeling feelings
I don't understand.

And worse: Sometimes I'm aware
of an ominous tick-tock
like a time bomb of hate,
set once and forgotten,
and a panic rises in my heart.

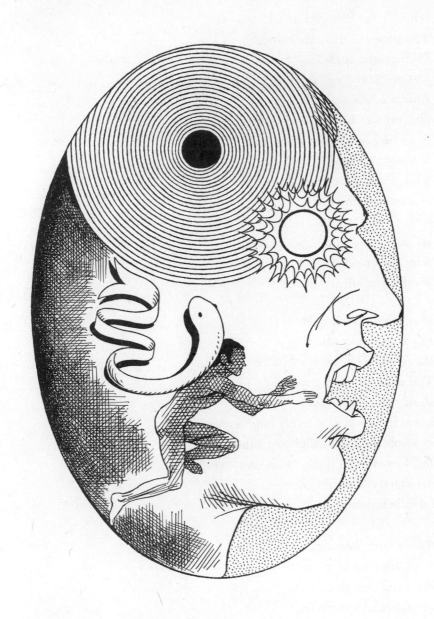

Then I try to think good thoughts
or take a bath
or walk around the block,
and if someone just frowns at me
I could wring their neck joyfully,
not that I would,
but the thought occurs to me.
So how can I trust my feelings
when I feel like that?"

The soul replies, "You must.
Your feelings are natural
as summer and winter,
sunshine and blizzards,
droughts and floods.
They are the natural elements
of the inner weather
that fill the fleshscape
of body and mind.

Dark, light,
threatening, joyful, angry —
your feelings are the colors,
the clouds, the mountains and valleys,
the deserts and lakes
of your inner world,
the bright scenes of your being,
flashing back and forth
through the meadow of your tissue
and the skies of your soul.

Your emotion is the light
that strikes and unites

113

both our worlds,
and is the path between
and the source of each,
for feeling is the power
out of which
all realities emerge."

The mortal self stops writing,
staring at the page
where in pen and ink
the soul just wrote its words
and says, "I didn't know.
I'm weak. Having held back
my feelings from myself for years,
I can hardly speak.
Besides, I thought you said before
that thoughts and beliefs
formed the life we know."

The soul replies,
"Your thoughts and beliefs
call up your feeling
and sculpt it into the image
of your conscious desire.
Ignore your feelings
and you're like a silly magician
who never knows what he'll pull out of his hat,
and never knows what to expect
because he doesn't understand
what he's working with,
and is afraid of the powers
his commands direct.
So tell me exactly what your feelings are
and we'll go on from there."

A Different Kind of Journey

Ah love this mortal self
who looks around nervously and says,
"I'm game but scared. All right,
I'll start by feeling
what I'm feeling now
as I look out the window.
Two pigeons just went sweeping by,
swooping through
the white pudding-thick sky.
I bet they didn't think
the day was dreary.
Why should I?

Yet on dark days like now
the color seems to drain
out of the world,
as if some magic's fled
and earth takes on the hues
of an afterlife or underworld,
as if its full brilliance
were forever gone.

Oh, out of which dimensions of my being
do the fragments fly
that fall headlong
into the jigsaw events
of my stained-glass days?
A dreary afternoon,
yet the birds aren't distorted

through my blue-stained eyes,
but they fly through the uncracked sky,
past the bare branches' edges
with an ease that makes me cry.

My feelings splash blue against the world,
yet its beauty seeps back in again
as my mood swoops through me
on its own wings,
like a wind falling to pieces
in the bottom of my soul.

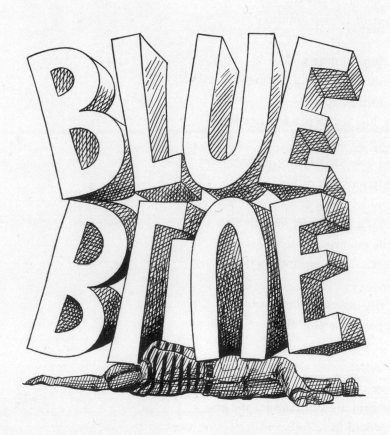

I plummet, dizzy, fascinated, frightened,
and find myself unbroken,
looking up at the world once more
like a bird just having landed
on the ground.

How feelings move if you let them!
That one sent me down invisible slides of tears
and I cried like a child, hanging on
but carried downward anyhow; scared,
to laugh at the bottom —
'Why, that wasn't so bad' —
and that mood, followed,
led me out of it into another.

And I felt you, dear soul,
in the rush of body and feeling and mind
all moving together.
My belly lurched as the feelings fell.
My scalp prickled.
Heat and cold swirled in my fingertips.
eddying in and out so fast
that I couldn't keep track.
I sobbed as a jay might screech,
out of the moment of itself
and you were that motion, swiftness,
all in me,
at once the journey of my being
and the power behind all.

A while ago
on feeling that panic
that just held me and then let me go,
I never would have followed it

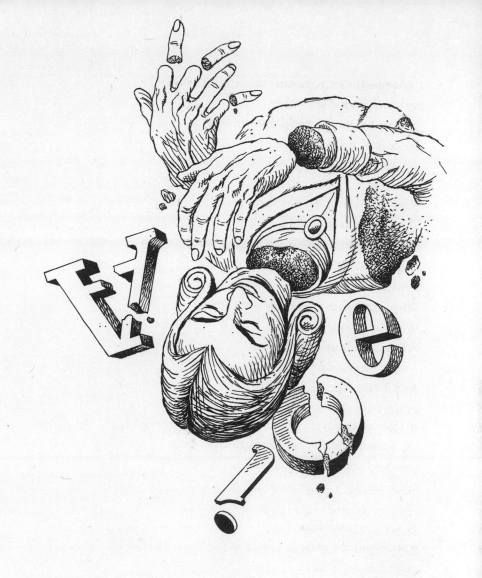

but quickly changed my thoughts
to something else,
and run as far as I could go
to get away from it.

But now
my body trembles and breathes deep.
Ancient angers
rumble up from my toes.
A dull heavy hole
rises up from my belly to my throat
and empties its load upon my tongue
which turns heavy
with unsaid, uncried things
long forgotten by my mind
but clotted in my blood.

Ashen statues
of unspoken vowels and syllables,
images I should have kicked,
all from my lips go toppling.

The specifics merge;
the icy leaden mass
grows alive in birth
and rushes, squalling
out into the universe.
Shapes and colors,
blacks and purples mix
with the skyscape's
great moving picture
and are lost
and redeemed in it.

I feel you now, even in my anger,
splendid and terrible,
emerging through my flesh
with the rightness of storm winds
and clouds blowing,
devastating the landscape
yet filling it with freshness,
sending debris flying
full blast, and releasing new tubers
which lay hidden under
and are justly served by my anger
which lifts them
and you and me altogether
over repression's frosty land,
surging in great free swirls
that burst like summer lightning, flashing
and speeding over the countryside,
joyously furious."

Pausing, the mortal self
takes a deep breath and says,
"Why did I feel that my anger
could unsettle the universe
or be so strong

121

that no one could stand
its simple utterance?
So I held all hurt inside
while my rage collected,
causing fault lines that crisscrossed
just beneath the surface
and cracked my days.

Why did the feelings of my creaturehood
stirring within me seem so strange?
Why did I deny the living expression
I envy in the animals?
What gentle summer storms did I repress
until finally
my body itself expressed
its fury that I
would diminish its dimensions
and dilute the heritage of blood?

What motion in me, now sensed,
rises in torrents of dissent
against denials I thought were right
and beliefs I held
until they nearly strangled
me to death?
Yet let me gently
lay them in the earth.
They thought they served me well
and I tended them with vigor
until now.

So let us hold
a funeral for old ideas.
I'll give them their proper merit,

speak
what gentle words I can
and let them go —
servants I let turn into masters,
bitter friends
I was loyal to till the end.

The dreams of my youth?
No. Those still live.
But the way I chose to achieve them
is dead, for they grew while I
kept trying to make them fit
a picture I'd painted years ago
and cried
because the painting came alive
and kept growing out of it.

It's the frame I have to throw away.
My living couldn't be
contained in it
and my beliefs held rigid,
squeezing my experience
in tiny smudges
so as not to run over the edges
into wilder dreams,
or add brilliant glazes
to the initial sketch beneath.

So dear ghosts, here assemble,
but not sadly.
I have to do the burying myself,
drop you one by one
into the springtime earth
where you can mix

freely with the elements,
become transformed
and find new birth
like Rooney
in a different kind
of consciousness.

Yet some part of me
dies with your death
and it's hard to say good-bye
to ghosts of yourself.
How many do we discard
so we can live?
Dear soul, I'm through.
It's done. The funeral
is over. I've cried
and brooded long enough.

I kept these feelings
like tiny creatures of their own,
locked up inside myself,
until they pawed and clawed
for their escape.
Just now I let them go,
and some more push up, run,
climb, fly,
a multitude headed up my vertebrae
at once,
sensing an open gate
like prisoners of war, suddenly released
after a hard-earned truce.

I'm swept along with them,
shouting freedom.
My thighs and chest
sing anthems as they pass
and my flesh becomes transformed,
what it is, and more,
its rich color-coated dreams
of touch and feelings
endow me with a life
in which my creaturehood
leaps beyond itself.

Now exultation builds,
a sudden arching river that roars
and spans both thought and sense.
It sweeps from some secret jubilation
of my genitals
and cascades through the valleys
of my brain.

Riding that joy, I look down
to see that my birth and death
both focus me in time, lest
I bleed outward at the edges
into the depths of All That Is
from which I came.
My birth — my death —
the emphatic definitions
that set my own living
apart from all others,
a kind gesture
to help me hold my uniqueness,

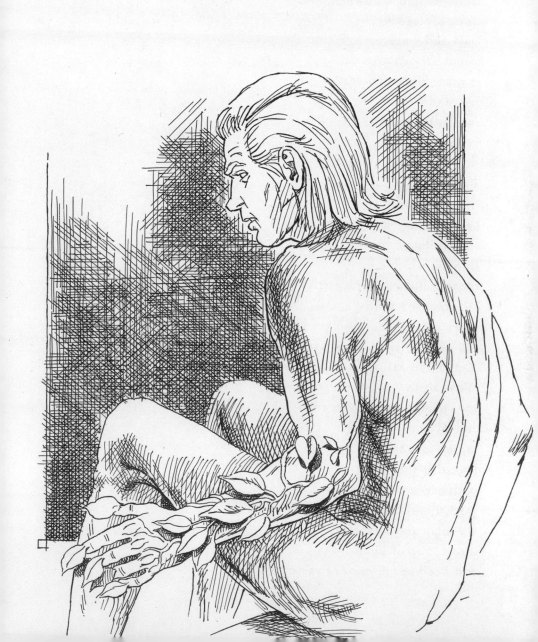

as night and day
focus me gently
between the sun's
coming and going.

But as I keep memory
from one day to another,
rising all together,
body and soul
to put fresh clothes on,
so other births and deaths
arrive to astonish me,
even as the seasons
vanish and return."

This moment, this hour
is like no other
because of my deaths and births
and the magic focus of the flesh
through which
the self intersects with earth
and knowing this,
transcends itself.

The mortal self, exhausted, sighs,
"What a trip
my feelings just took me on,
and all
in one afternoon.
I see that they unite
both our worlds.
But what about that light I saw
the night the puddle turned
into a lung of light
and stood up, all made of rain?"

The soul replies
"Because you were so mental,
we had to deal with words —
hence these dialogues.
And so you saw the light outside of yourself
and didn't feel it with your flesh,
or sense its source
as the living glow that penetrates
our double worlds,
the light of life that moves and flows
and can't be stopped or stilled."

The mortal self sighs again
and pets the cat
and lights a cigarette,
then says, "Dear soul,
then I didn't really want to be
of this world. How odd.
God knows where I wanted to be
instead.
Not dead, that's sure.
But I tried to lose my body in my head
and thus lose time and pain and death
and nearly lost myself instead.
So I return
to the sanity of the animals'
miraculous commotion in space and time."

PART SIX

Occult Spring

Occult Spring

Ah listen,
as soul and mortal self
like vowels and consonants
utter together
the magic syllables
that form the self in flesh,
and speak
the language
of their single-double worlds.
They merge
as they were always merged in one,
the soul alive in creaturehood
and the mortal self
emerging out of soul
endlessly creating itself.

The mortal self says, "Dear soul,
thanks for the lessons.
I know our dialogues are through,
and in a way, I'm sad.
But is there anything
you want to add?"

The soul smiles
and shakes its head,
heartily says, "Amen,"
and disappears
within itself.

The next day the mortal self
sits down to work as usual,
but now looking out the window, feels
soul and self as one,
perceiving their joint
morning universe,
and says—

"What liquid sounds the birds make
this first March morning;
their warbling wiggles and ripples
like blue-green ribbons
flowing through the bare branches, forming
rivers of sound
that invisibly splash against my ear
and brush against my cheek which rises up
like a shining cliff of coral,
fleshy chips merged,
but soft and glistening.

The fir tree branches
wave like seaweed,
so that even the house next door
seems like a cliff dwelling underground,
the air soft, yet cold
as the ocean in the morning.

Cars go by like swift fish
with giant fins,
tossing waves of sound
up past second-story windows
where they fall back in smooth folds
into the street again.

My cat looks out the window.
Ten o'clock
and the day itself grows full
with its own support,
oddly mysterious
and, if you'll forgive the term,
occult.

For beneath it all, some ancient
yet new
stirring rises everywhere,
unseen but felt,
perceived by the animals.
Some message rustles the air,
making peaks and valleys in it,
opening up
fields of space
that weren't there before.

Is Rooney, my dead cat, aware of it?
How kind the earth,
tucking itself into his bones
so that his tongue
lies flat
and flower seeds will speak
their growing up from it.
But even that cat corpse turns,
listens, trembles, moves,
and pours itself into life again,
sending miniature dirt slides
in the earth piles shuddering.

A sliver of a bone falls,
is swallowed by a living root
and turns
with new agility through the smooth
undersides of the universe.
And each part of any corpse
that once flew or walked the earth
now in its way hears
messages rising from its dreaming roots.

What are the secrets
of the seance rooms to compare with this —
wholesale new worlds
emerging from twig;
frogs
looking through a collie's eyes
as he rushes through
springtime backyards?

Occult spring
brings the dead to life
with her spells.
What conjuring
calls the sudden apport
of leaves
that will appear bursting
with their tiny tender green spangles
shaking,
quaking their fresh banners
on branches now
thin and bare as wires?

The secret cabinets of earth
begin to open.
All the intimate commotions
of moon and sun's alliance grew
until the earth itself
bursts wide
and the underground lives;
millions of tiny rich dirt doors
flying out into the sunlight
and the new fruits,
resplendent,
rise from the cellar stores
of desire
that lay hidden
beneath the winter snow.

Three o'clock.
Lunch come and gone.
I've read the letters
that came to me by mail,
but still
those other messages
go swirling
through the afternoon.
A jay's throat moves
and corporal ecstasy
rides
the sky for blocks.
Invisible to me, that jay,
yet I believe
because I've heard.

A squirrel
looks in the window at me.
What contact is between us?
We both heard the jay
and feel in our own way
the passive thrusting
motion of the day's
rise and fall,
and sense
the messages that make
him part human
and me
part squirrel.

The cells in these hands might well have blown
through the eyes with which that squirrel
looks at me now,
and the atoms within my skin
might yesterday
have formed his fur.
Yet separate and apart,
each of us watches
the other through the glass.

A pause.
The old man next door
takes out his garbage. He walks
so smoothly
through the stretched-out air
that he might as well
be gliding.

The sun, just then,
splashes out its sudden light,
startling,
and the fir tree branches quicken.

My heart rises
like the pigeon that just flew
to the chimney
and my throat flutters
as his wings do.
I almost catch
the messages.
My hands feel silky, soft and warm;
liquidy.
I could slip them off, it seems,
yet watch them lift up
my solid coffee cup
and then dance
up and down on the right
typewriter keys,
like ten
birds changing places
on a tree.

The sky darkens.
Where the old man walked
there is an empty shadow,
and the pigeon's gone.
The fir tree just quieted,
its branches poised,
relaxed and loose
in the darker, stiller air.

Yet my face is flushed
as if the sun
disappeared inside my skin
and turned
my insides into flowing gold,
not cold
but warm and glowing.
My spine prickles and I think
of myself cooking supper
and people
returning home to lighted kitchens,
riding the currents
of the afternoon
to their evening destinations,
all secret,
knowing and unknowing,
feeling
beneath their coming and their going
the occult stirrings
of their blood.

While we eat our supper,
within the moist dirt outside,
hidden in darkness,
a million slender shoots are rising
as clairvoyant spring
prepares her latest
demonstration.
What a public display,
as every day flashes
once more
eternal!